Peter Gill

Peter Gill was born in 1939 in Cardiff and started his
professional career as an actor. A director as well as a
writer, he has directed over eighty productions in the
UK, Europe and North America. At the Royal Court
Theatre in the sixties, he was responsible for introducing
D. H. Lawrence's plays to the theatre. The founding
director of Riverside Studios and the Royal National
Theatre Studio, Peter Gill lives in London. His plays
include *The Sleepers Den* (Royal Court, London, 1965),
Over Gardens Out (Royal Court, London, 1968), *Small
Change* (Royal Court, London, 1976), *Kick for Touch*
(National Theatre, London, 1983), *Cardiff East* (National
Theatre, London, 1997), *Certain Young Men* (Almeida
Theatre, 1999), *The York Realist* (English Touring Theatre,
2001) and *Original Sin* (Sheffield Crucible, 2002).

D1556628

PETER GILL

Another Door Closed

faber and faber

First published in 2009
by Faber and Faber Limited
74–77 Great Russell Street, London WC1B 3DA

Typeset by Country Setting, Kingsdown, Kent CT14 8ES
Printed and bound in Great Britain by CPI Antony Rowe

A CIP record for this book is available
from the British Library

978–0–571–25478–1

2 4 6 8 10 9 7 5 3 1

Another Door Closed was first presented by the Peter Hall Company at the Theatre Royal, Bath, on 4 August 2009. The cast was as follows:

Woman One June Watson
Woman Two Marjorie Yates
Man Sean Chapman

Director Peter Gill
Designer Jessica Curtis
Lighting Designer Paul Pyant
Sound Designer Marcus Christensen
Composer Christian Mason
Casting Director Amy Ball

Characters

Woman One
Woman Two
Man

ANOTHER DOOR CLOSED

*The layout of the dialogue is not intended
to be prescriptive. It does not indicate
a system of pauses or silences, but is there
to make for easier reading and to give some
general indication of rhythm and flow.*

*Front door favouring upstage right. Square on.
Back door downstage left. Door up and downstage.
Living room centre.*

SCENE ONE

Woman One, inside the closed front door, facing front holding two shopping bags.

Woman Two, sitting facing the open back door.

Woman One
 Are you there, dear?

Woman Two
 Is that you, dear?

Woman One
 Are you there, dear? Are you in?

Woman Two
 Yes, dear.

Woman One
 It's me, dear.

 Are you there, dear? Are you in, dear?

Woman Two
 I'm here, dear.

Woman One
 Are you in? Are you there, dear?

Woman Two
 Yes, dear. I'm here dear. Are you in?

Woman One
 Are you?

 Are you in? Oo-oo. Are you there?

Woman Two
I'm here dear.

Woman One
Are you?

Are you?

Are you?

Woman Two
I'm here dear. I'm here dear. Yes, dear.

I'm here with you in this lovely light, throwing bread crumbs through the back door for the birds.

Woman One
Are you?

Woman Two
I'm here throwing bread crumbs through the back door for the birds.

Woman One
Through the window for the birds.

Woman Two
Through the back door for the birds.

For the robin and the blackbird.

Bread crumbs from the bread board thrown out the back door for the birds.

Woman One
Through the window.

Woman Two
For the robin and the blackbird.

Perhaps I can tempt them in.

Woman One
Not through the window?

Woman Two
No, dear, through the door.

We are lucky dear, here, dear.

Woman One
Yes, dear.

Woman Two
Are you in now, dear?

Woman One
I am, dear.

Woman Two
Good, dear. I'm glad, dear.

Woman One
Is it nice? The garden, looking nice?

Woman Two
It is, dear.

Woman One
Is anyone there dear, in the garden?

Woman Two
Through the back door for the robin.

Woman One
Is there?

Is Mother in the garden? Is she? Is she, dear, in the garden?

Woman Two
They might come hopping in.

Woman One
Tell me if she is?

Woman Two
Through the back door up and on to the window sill and that way free into the garden again.

Woman One
Is she pegging out the clothes?

Woman Two
Tempt them in.

Woman One
Is she in the garden, is she? Is she pulling up the line? Are the sheets high in the wind, is she looking up at the sheets high up against the sky?

Woman Two
Tempt them in with these fresh crumbs.

Woman Onc
Is she chatting over the fence?

Woman Two
The birds.

Woman One
Is she cutting back the lilac, is she?

Where is she then?

Is she in the house? Is she in the house then? Is she upstairs, making the beds? Is she opening the curtains, turning out a cupboard, folding the sheets, is she?

Is she on the landing, looking out, looking through the window, is she? Looking out waiting for us to come home?

Is she waiting for us to come home? Are we running home, running home in our ribbons?

Woman Two
There's a cat in the garden.

Woman One

Is she? Is she scrubbing the steps, polishing the sideboard?

Woman Two

The cat might eat the birds.

Woman One

Is she downstairs then?

Woman Two

Not our cat. Whose cat?

Woman One

Blackleading the grate?

Woman Two

We don't have a cat.

Woman One

Downstairs, taking out the ashes?

Woman Two

Or a dog, now.

Woman One

Doing the washing?

Is she counting the Kunzle cakes? Skimming the stew, bottling the fruit, making her puddings, tying up parcels, heeling the socks?

Is she? Is she there?

Is there spring in the sofa, salt in the jar, suet in the pudding, the dripping on the toast, the wood in the hole, the fat in the fire, the nigger in the woodpile? Are there enough darning needles? Is there buckram and butter muslin?

Oh, where is she, dear, if she's not there?

Woman Two
Little Jack when he was a puppy, he used to cry at night like a baby.

Woman One
Is she, dear? Is she?

Tell me. Is she? Tell me, dear.

Woman Two
I don't think so, dear.

Woman One
No.

Woman Two
I don't think so.

Woman One
No.

Woman Two
It doesn't seem so.

Woman One
Oh dear.

Woman Two
Come in then now, dear. Take your coat off, dear.

Woman One
Yes. Thank you, dear.

Woman Two
Come in, dear.

Woman One
She's not there then, you say.

Woman Two
No.

Come in dear now.

Woman One
Yes.

She's not there then. You can close the door then. You can close the door now, I'm here. You can close the door. Stop that now, dear. It's time to come in now, dear. She's not here dear, dear, is she?

All that fuss, all that fuss, all that fuss.

She's not there now, is she?

Woman Two
No dear, I thought you would know she was not there.

She was not here.

Woman One
You can close the door now.

Looking out the door for the birds, looking into the fire. I'll bring these in. You can close it now.

Woman Two
I will dear, directly.

Dear?

Woman One
Yes dear?

Woman Two
Dear?

Woman One
Yes dear?

Woman Two
Will there be pain?

Woman One
Close it now, dear.

Woman Two
Will there be time, dear?

Woman One
I expect so, dear.

Woman Two
Will I have time?

Woman One
Time, dear, for what?

Woman Two
To finish my work.

Woman One
I should think so, dear.

Close the door dear now, I'm here, dear.

Woman Two
Close, close.

Woman One
Good, that's good, that's good.

Woman Two
Are you coming in, dear?

Woman One
I am in, dear.

SCENE TWO

Woman Two standing, her hand on the back door handle.

Woman Two
Are you there, dear?

Are you?

Is she there?

Dear?

Are you in, dear?

Close it. Close the door then.

Shall I, dear, close it then? Close it, she says. Close it.

Are you?

Close it against the birds. Against the cat that steals
the fish, the cat that is not there now.

And she is not there. She is not there. She is putting
the things away, is she?

She is so good. You are so good so good to me.

Are you there, dear?

SCENE THREE

Woman One standing in the living room.

Woman One

Are you coming in, dear?

Shall I make the tea now, dear? Or shall you?

Shall I lay the cloth?

SCENE FOUR

*Woman Two standing, her hand on the back door
handle.*

Woman Two

Close, close the door then.

*As she closes the back door, the front door opens.
As if in reaction to this, she opens the back door
again seeming to make the front door close in time
with it. This is repeated until the front door wins the
struggle and the Man stands in front of the closed
front door.*

Man
Hello.

SCENE FIVE

The Man and the two Women in the living room.

Man
So this is where you came?

Woman One
Do we know you?

Man
How long have you been here?

Woman One
Do we know him? Do we know you?

Man
Has it been for long? How long has it been? Has it
been long? Strange if it has been.

Woman One
What does he want? Who is he? Ask him.

Woman Two
I don't know, I don't know.

Woman One
Can we help you? Is there something you want?

Man
Strange for me, this. It's hard to take in.

I took it for granted that you would be there still. Why wouldn't you be?

Not prepared, not prepared at all, you know, for it all to be gone like that.

Woman One
Who is he?

Ask him, dear.

Woman Two
You ask him.

Man
It's gone, it's gone, you know, your house. Well, of course, you must know. It's all gone all down there. All of it.

Has she gone?

Of course, of course, that's it, isn't it?

Woman One
How did he get in? Do we know him?

Woman Two
I don't know. I closed the door . . .

Man
It's a shock.

Woman One
Who is he?

Woman Two
Ask him.

Woman One
Who is he? Who are you?

Man

All gone. It's all gone. All gone.

Woman Two

I thought he must have come about some repair, to do some work, some fixing of something.

Woman One

Don't be so silly. He hasn't come about a repair. It's obvious that he hasn't. It's quite clear that he hasn't.

Woman Two

How is it clear? I thought that's why he might have come. Though we don't need any work done, as far as I know.

Do we need something done?

Man

Don't you know me? No, of course you don't. You don't know me. Do you? You don't remember, do you? Guess, go on. You remember. No.

Woman Two

We really don't need anything done, you see.

Woman One

He hasn't come to do anything. What's the matter with you? You can see that. Anyone could see that.

Woman Two

He might have come for that. He looks as if he could have come for that.

Woman One

Really, dear.

Woman Two

Well, don't scold.

Woman One

Well, really.

Woman Two

Well, I know.

Woman One

But do you know?

Woman Two

But we have wanted someone to look at the boiler, before any hard weather. It would be prudent, as a precaution. You said so yourself.

Woman One

There's nothing wrong with the boiler.

Woman Two

But as a precaution, you said.

Woman One

Be quiet and ask him what he wants.

Woman Two

Well, now he is here . . . And who would we get now, if we needed someone, if the roof leaked? You won't send for Mr Franks.

Woman One

Don't worry about the roof now.

Woman Two

I am worried about it.

Woman One

There is no need to, dear.

Woman Two

I know and you are so handy. She is so handy. You are, dear. So handy. I must think of that.

But not to go on the roof, dear.

Woman One

There is no need for anyone to go on the roof or to look at the boiler or to fix the guttering or to do anything else. There is nothing wrong. Everything is fine. You are silly.

Woman Two

But he could look, dear, now he's here. Perhaps you would look for us? So kind.

And we could put the kettle on and make a cup of tea, dear.

Or you could have glass of beer. Beer? Or tea, have tea, or could he have a glass of beer? We kept beer for Mr Franks who used to come, who doesn't come any more, while you look.

Woman One

She is like some people are with babies.

Man

You don't know me, do you? Don't you know me? Don't you remember me? Of course, things move on. You have moved on. Of course.

And there's nothing there, you know, nothing at all down there now, you know. Well, you know. Nothing. Just waste land.

But why did you come here? Why here? How did you choose here? Hard to choose, I should think after that . . . But here, this is quite . . . It's different. Isn't it? Couldn't be more. Nothing at all you know. No feeling of anything that was . . . Quite different, strange.

She's gone. Tell me she has gone. I know, I can tell.

Woman One

Don't say anything, dear, until we know who he is.

Woman Two

But he knows us, dear.

Woman One
He presumes to know us.

Woman Two
Perhaps we know him. It would follow.

Woman One
If we do know him. Do you know him?

Woman Two
He seems to know us.

Man
She wouldn't have been happy here, would she?

Woman Two
Who do you mean?

Man
Who do I mean? Who do I mean?

Would she?

Woman One
Go now. Thank you, thank you very much.

Woman Two
Yes, go.

Man
There's nothing of her here, no feel of her. Would she be happy here? I ask you? This is not right for her here. I don't think so, do you?

Woman Two
Why not? Why not?

Woman One
Now, dear. No.

Woman Two
Why wouldn't she like it here? How do you know that?

Woman One

Be quiet. Don't say any more, now.

Man

I thought that it might be different. That it would have to be, when I found that you had gone. But not as much as this.

Are you different too? I think you are. I can feel it. You're different. No offence. Thank you for your time.

Do you want me to go now, do you? Shall I go now?

She isn't here, is she? No. It's true. That's it and I thought she might be. But she isn't.

I'll go now.

Why are you so cold?

I brought something for her, as I always used to long ago whenever I came back. A gift. I brought her a gift.

I would have brought her endless gifts.

What interest am I to you? I know. I was no interest to you then. No, never. Why should you care about my grief, this grief now? There is no obligation. You aren't obliged to me.

What are you worried about? There is no harm intended. You see, I didn't bargain for this. I had no idea it would all be gone. You see. It's left me . . . well . . .

I was so certain she would be there. She was constant you see, in my mind. Even though of course sometimes I had thoughts of the worst, that perhaps she wouldn't still be there, after all. It's always fear amidst fantasy when you are away for so long and so far, but it's a comfort, in your loneliness, to dream of someone constant, in your exile. The thought of her always bright in my mind then, for I was away for so long, you see.

This return is . . . well, it's, look, it's not of any consequence is it? This return. You have to have imagination to epic it, this return to her, to pay court to, at least to where she was.

I thought . . . But now. She isn't here, is she? Too late. Shall I go?

Woman One

Yes, go now.

Woman Two

Best you do now, I think.

Man

Is that what you want, is it?

Have you grown hard? Is that it? You were never hard then, you know. Just two spoiled daughters. Two little, selfish daughters. Two unemancipated daughters. Without her you have become hard, is that it? She was so soft, you see.

I am loyal to her you see, utterly, always.

This wasn't the right place for her. That's a comfort, that is.

I didn't think of you once, you know. Of course. There was only her, you should know that. Who am I kidding? You're too spoiled, you are, to think that I would have. Except to think how important you were, tangentially, implicitly, by reason of who you were and because of how important you were tangentially, implicitly. I thought of you sometimes. And now things have moved on, is that it? And you have become hard?

But admit it, admit that I was never of interest to you. Though I was always interested you know in your perfect-little-woman lives, that had no scope. You were never interested in me, never. You don't remember. Remembering me is not important to you. I'll go.

Woman One
Yes.

Woman Two
Poor man.

Woman One
I'm not taken in.

Man
I'll go.

Woman Two
No, stay with us and talk then.

Woman One
No, dear.

Woman Two
Oh let him stay, dear.

Stay now, is it?

Let him talk and tell and we will listen.

Woman One
But that won't be the end of it. I know how it will be. If we let him stay now, that will be it, I know.

You will ply him with questions and he will ask things of us in return. That's how it will be. We have found how it is with you dear, with you, always. And you only wanting to be nice and the next thing, the house is full of them.

Like Mother, you – house full of strangers popping in nosing, wanting to know everything, the ins and outs. You ask him how is your wife, you ask after the children – that happened with Mr Franks. Then the birthdays, the children's birthdays and cutting out of newspapers and recipes. It is too taxing.

And there is always an interpretation of things, of personal things. You will be telling him things, birth signs, private things. But it's too much now, dear. I had to put a stop to it with Mr Franks.

Woman Two
We won't talk of anything that doesn't suit you. But it's nice to talk and it won't be about us, dear, he won't want to talk about us, they never do.

He will want to talk about Mother. Except Mr Franks who liked us, but he doesn't come any more.

Woman One
These people, always asking for her as if she wasn't our concern and we were of no consequence.

Woman Two
We must be hospitable, dear, to the stranger at the gate. Mother would like it don't you think?

Woman One
Too much. It's too much.

Woman Two
I know, dear. But it was always worth it, to please her.

Woman One
Oh dear. Why did you let him in?

Woman Two
I know I know.

I closed the door. I closed the door and I closed the door and another one opened.

Woman One

Dear, dear.

The Man is crying.

Woman Two

He's crying. He's put a handkerchief to his eyes, crying.

When a man cries, oh – dear.

Woman One

The enchantment of men.

Man

It's gone the other house the house I knew so well the house where she was queen where she was kind to me always, and bathed my face when I had a fall.

Woman Two

Oh we don't think of it, do we? Time in the other house never.

Woman One

She bathed your face.

Man

And called me her little soldier. And it's gone the haven in my childhood.

You remember me. Don't you know me?

Woman Two

We welcome you to our home.

Man

But don't you hold it in your heart the good fortune you had in those times there with her?

I saw you with a child's eye, wondering at the immensity of your good fortune.

Your grandfather's house and you were little girls with ribbons and white dresses at first and then young ladies in waisted costumes and hats and gloves. La-di-dah la-di-dah. There down by the river with horses loose on the bank, the tinker's horses. You were young ladies when I last saw you, in hats and gloves.

Woman Two

He remembers us as little girls with ribbons.

Woman One

We were little girls with ribbons, dear.

Man

Little girls, all ribbons, in your grandfather's pony and trap.

Woman Two

That was long ago.

Man

Doesn't it mean what it means to me?

Woman One

We only think of this house. That was another house. Not our house as this is ours, you see.

Woman Two

Yes, this is our home. This is our home.

Man

Wasn't that your home?

Woman Two

For years now this is our home.

Woman One

Don't speak of it. You see why he asks. It's not for us, never for us. We are of no interest to you. You visit us as if we were in another country and you were a traveller looking in.

Man

I was her cavalier. It's a tribute to her that I am here.

Woman Two

Shall I make tea? Shall I? Or get him a beer? Mr Franks liked beer. We liked to spoil him. Kept a beer for him after hard work.

Woman One

It will start with a beer.

Woman Two

But you liked Mr Franks. You ascertained his taste in beer. It was you found out that he liked beer and which beer. It was important to you to do the right thing. And it was you who stopped him coming.

Woman One

It will develop. I know it. I know you.

Woman Two

Or would you prefer tea?

Man

Thank you for inviting me into your home, such kindness.

Woman One

It is the thing to do.

Woman Two

Or would he like a beer?

Man

And I've brought . . . a thing, something.

Woman One

Shall I make tea or get him a beer? Shall I?

Woman Two
Get him a beer.

Let me get it.

SCENE SIX

The two Women alone.

Woman One
There is no beer. I will lay a cloth for tea.

Why did you let him in? We will have to go over all that now. Talk about all that now.

Woman Two
Only for politeness dear, to be nice. Don't you think? To listen, after he has been such a long time away, he says. It will be a kindness. Are you sure there is none?

Woman One
None that I could see.

Woman Two
In the larder there should be some.

Woman One
All that brought up now.

Woman Two
I know. But not for long, it won't be for long.

Woman One
I don't want it. I don't want to hear it all again. How can we get rid of him? You must get rid of him.

Woman Two
It will be all right. We won't go beyond the bounds of courtesy, dear.

Woman One

But I haven't the energy for it. You have such energy, dear, for it, for callers, for making tea for the builder, for how-is-it-coming-along to the workman, for how-is-your-wife to them – your son.

You find romance in it all. You would make tea for strangers, for the people passing by in the street, call them in off the street, as if they were the vicar, calling by appointment, if I let you. You would. You would call in strangers.

Woman Two

It is my way, dear. You make too much of it. You do.

Not tea but tea and biscuits, not tea and biscuits but you must make the biscuits, not make the biscuits but make the bread for the bread and butter that you think would be nice for the little sandwiches that you make and caster sugar for the sponge cake that you bake.

Men are more rough and ready dear, and too much fuss unnerves them, if they notice, that's if they notice anything at all.

You turn things into such a task. It exhausts you and it exhausts the men, dear, too I'm afraid. They like a quiet life on their own terms.

Woman One

And that's my way, dear.

Woman Two

I see, dear. Don't be nasty, dear.

Woman One

Yes, dear. Mother's politeness, dear. You say so yourself. It costs nothing.

Where is he gone?

Woman Two

He won't be long. We'll be polite. Entertain him and then he'll leave in good time, you'll see.

Woman One

Are you sure he will leave in good time?

Woman Two

I'll make sure he leaves. You'll see. I can do that.

Woman One

But will you? It's too much, a total stranger calling and then implying intimacy. Too much, too near.

Woman Two

He's not really a total stranger, dear. We knew him, dear. You know that don't you dear, he's not a total stranger is he?

Woman One

I don't know that he isn't, really.

Woman Two

We owe him the time of day at least.

Don't you remember? You must remember him.

Woman One

Of course I do, yes of course I do.

But why do we owe him anything at all? I don't owe him. Do you think that you owe him?

Woman Two

He didn't mean a lot to me, that boy.

Woman One

Nor to me.

He seems to have made a lot of a little, as far as I can see.

Woman Two

He used to come down on a Sunday.

Woman One

He did.

You would remember him, you have a fondness for remembering things.

Woman Two

But I haven't remembered him and remembered with any longing. I haven't said, 'Oh do you remember that boy, that, that woman's boy, that Mother took a fancy to, I wonder how he is or is he thinking of us?' I haven't done that.

Woman One

I barely remember him at all. He was forgotten.

Woman Two

You know who he is of course, whose son he is, of course?

Woman One

Of course. Of course I do. Of course I know. Really dear.

Woman Two

All the more reason for politeness.

Woman One

Why?

Woman Two

Not to show it mattered to us.

Woman One

But it did matter to us. It did then to Mother. It did.

Woman Two

But not show it as she didn't show it.

Woman One

To as it were wet our knickers and hide the fact.

Woman Two

That was you dear, to wet your knickers and hide the fact.

Woman One

Wet knickers are often a fact of life.

Woman Two

But best to keep quiet about them then.

Woman One

I wish he was gone, dear.

Woman Two

Don't, dear. Why are you so worried?

Woman One

I can't put up with anyone, dear, only you, dear. It's so exhausting. I am exhausted by the prospect. Get rid of him. What does he want? Won't you?

Woman Two

I think he is just making connections, you know. Not much more than that. It won't be long, just a visit, remember.

After his mother died, Father took an interest in him for some reason.

Woman One

For some reason. Really, what a thing to say.

Woman Two

After his mother died.

Woman One

For some reason, for some reason.

Woman Two
Well, I know.

Woman One
And mother with a kind of ferocity all of her own decided to be kind to him because he was the son of that woman. That was typical of her indiscriminate compassion, and her way of reckoning, of understanding. Because he was that woman's son.

Woman Two
Well, she would reason that it was not his fault.

Woman One
But we have no such peculiar obligation to him.

Woman Two
Well, Father had some duty, some obligation to him certainly or felt he had in part because she was married to his old friend. That was at the root of it.

Father got him a place on a ship. He went to sea. Father advised.

Woman One
And what about his obligation to Mother? Obligation to an old friend. Obligation indeed to the old friend's wife.

Woman Two
He went to her funeral.

Woman One
I remember.

Woman Two
Of a broken heart do you think? She . . .

Woman One
You are a storyteller.

Woman Two
Well, she must have been quite young.

Woman One
Mother brushed his hat and you polished his shoes.

Woman Two
That was what I always did. Did I not?

Woman One
Yes dear.

Woman Two
He would always come on a Sunday. Mother liked him. The big tea on Sunday when you baked. Though we had little to do with him. A favourite with Mother. Waifs and strays always with her.

Woman One
Because of Father, to manage Father.

Woman Two
That was her way. One of the many characters in the house as it was then.

Woman One
But now we have our own life. We have forgotten all that.

Woman Two
It comes back. It comes back.

Woman One
But to bid it to come. And this reminder of father's peccadilloes. It would be loyal to Mother to have nothing to do with him, that boy.

Woman Two
He said it was his duty, his duty to go. She was married to his old friend. He said that was the reason.

Woman One

For she was one of the many.

Woman Two

I think of the many, the one.

Woman One

But he came back, she always had him back. He always came back.

Woman Two

Always had him back till the end.

Woman One

You nursed him in the end, dear.

Woman Two

Of course, dear. But you, he always asked for you, dear.

Woman One

Oh, let's not give him the time.

Woman Two

He was only a man.

Woman One

What is that, what is that?

Woman Two

You are hard on men, dear.

Woman One

I can do without them.

Woman Two

Mother could wind you round her finger, she expected things of you, had high hopes.

That you would become a secretary.

Woman One

Anyway that is all over now, all over now.

Woman Two
It's as if you didn't like him dear, Father.

Woman One
He didn't like me. He was irritated by me. I irritated him like an itch.

There was always awkwardness. You were his beloved. He laughed at your little monkey ways.

Don't let's give him the time.

Woman Two
Really, darling.

Woman One
All this unravelling. And now a present. He brought her a present.

Woman Two
But it's nothing new to us, dear. Often when we were young Grandfather's clients, his customers, his callers, whatever they were, they would bring us little treasures from journeys abroad.

Now shall you make the tea then or shall I?

Woman One
I'll make it.

SCENE SEVEN

The Man and the two Women looking at a little box.

Woman One
What is this?

Man
Open it.

Woman Two
Look, dear.

Woman One
Well, he gave it to you.

Woman Two
Well, I know.

Man
Jealousy?

Woman One
No, none, is there?

Woman Two
No, no.

Man
No sisterly rivalry?

Woman One
Not worthy of an answer.

Woman Two
What a lovely thing, this box.

Woman One
Well, open it.

Woman Two
Wouldn't you like to?

Woman One
Open it.

Woman Two
What is in it?

She opens it.

Woman Two
Look, dear, so lovely.

Woman One
  Show me.

Woman Two
  What is it?

Man
  It's jade.

Woman Two
  Is it jade?

Woman One
  Yes, it's jade.

Man
  Chinese jade.

Woman Two
  Oh dear, this is a beautiful thing. Was it for . . .?

Man
  Yes. Always for her. For you now. It's pure. From the mountains and the lakes. You have it now.

Woman Two
  Oh no, we couldn't. But it is lovely.

Woman One
  Yes, give it back. Put it in the box.

  Give it to me. Take it please.

Woman Two
  We can't, you see.

Man
  Please, it was for her.

Woman One
  But who would wear it, you see?

Man
Both of you I hope, now.

Woman Two
Oh, no.

Woman One
And there you have it.

Woman Two
It is a beautiful thing.

Woman One
You have it.

Woman Two
Oh no, dear.

Woman One
We look forward to heaven when these things will be settled.

Woman Two
In the way of settling, you see, things we would both have one, you see then, so there was no rivalry. Things were settled so well. That was the way then.

Man
Don't you really miss it? A place where returning men brought gifts, when jade was the order of things?

Woman One
You have a memory of it different to ours.

Man
Don't you miss it, your grandfather's house where you lived for so long? Where he kept his business.

What did he do there, was the little shop, was it a front? But for what? The little bit of chandlering, fronting something of the this and that. The house a front for his dealings in cash, for his little fiddle?

Don't you miss it? A house full of treasure, filled as if with booty, with too much furniture with cane chairs and iron-bound trunks and pistols on the wall and sailing ships in cases. The house filled with too much, with fans and boxes of moths and butterflies and lace and embroidered cloths and kimonos, and watches stopped.

Your mother kept a good house for him. Where he treated your father like a prince with his black horse and your old granny like a gypsy woman behind the counter at the front. And him with his strong cigarettes and his black coffee in a copper jug.

Woman Two
Grandfather's cousin who helped him with his books.

Man
With her long lobes pulled down with gold earrings. Sitting with him in the saloon where they would both work, he sitting at his big roll-topped desk in the saloon. Lending to the poor sailors high and dry after cashing their notes and all his little deals and his Bible and the big flagged kitchen floor, and the motley of things and bibelots filling it up. A wondrous place where he gave me sixpence and your father was the prince and she washed my face, not your granny.

Woman Two
Father's cousin.

Man
She was a rancorous old thing with her crocodile tears worshipping the men and undermining your mother, who was the real queen, the empress there, and you with your compacts and face powder and piano lessons.

I sent cards to her from all my trips and she stuck
them into a mirror.

Woman One
Have you a mole?

Man
I have a mole.

Woman One
Mother said she . . . you could tell by that.

I will make the tea.

Woman Two
Or beer dear, would you like a beer? I am sure there is
beer dear, you haven't looked everywhere. Are we
sure?

SCENE EIGHT

The Man and Woman Two.

Woman Two
She's making the tea.

Man
Thank you.

Woman Two
I know that we have beer but we can't seem to find it.
I thought we kept it in the larder.

Man
Oh, well.

Woman Two
So we'll lay tea in here.

Man
You try to make things easy, is that it?

38

Woman Two

I don't know what you mean.

Man

You ease things? Is that what you do?

Woman Two

This is so pretty.

Man

Put it on.

Woman Two

Oh, dear no. I couldn't. It wouldn't do. No.

Man

I like women in pretty things.

Do you wear gloves as a matter of course? Do you wear a hat to show off your face? I don't suppose that you do, now.

Woman Two

We wear gloves against the cold. Of course we do.

Man

What kind of gloves?

Woman Two

Woollen gloves for the warmth.

Man

Not kid gloves? Not soft leather gloves or crocheted gloves that are open, to show off your beautiful hands in the summer?

Woman Two

Are you still sad?

Man

I'm disappointed, of course I am. But I'll have to get over that. Even if you were prepared for disappointment, you can never be reconciled to it at first, if ever, I think now in this case.

Reality has hit me in the face. It can be such a very lacklustre thing, can't it? But you have made it easier, I must say. I wasn't prepared for the extent of it, of the change in everything, you see. In you. Or are my expectations beyond reasonable? I must get used to it I suppose.

Woman Two
What has most changed?

Man
The look of you. You have moved on and now it is as if your femininity was something not worth holding on to. Is it all beneath you? Is it the frills, the prettiness, the ribbons?

Woman Two
What do you mean?

Man
I have been where the understanding of femininity is profound. Where they understand something deep about men and about women, some men, most men. Where they understand something about femininity, about women and where it lands, femininity lands, how it lands. And there is an understanding then of the role of gender and its mysterious transferable power. How the fake can be more than the real.

There is magic in dress. Perception can get to the heart of things. There is a profound difference between men and women at the heart of this matter and yet the apparent rules are there to be broken. A woman who has many pairs of shoes knows something that is more than show, that is an understanding of this. There is magic in outward signs as there is in all that can be underneath, stockings, underpinnings, all that can be underneath, all of it augmented by the smell.

It's a mistake you know if you're a woman to dress for other women. Good taste is a mistake. A woman should risk being ludicrous if she is to dress right.

She judged it you see perfectly, in a way that couldn't be faked. You have settled for the second division. Haven't you?

She left us alone clearly. Are we to act upon that, do you think? What is the significance? Is there a probationary element? I am bound to take advantage.

Woman Two

How would you take advantage?

Man

That would be up to you.

It's an opportunity. For you to try on the necklace is what I mean, do you think you would like to try it now? Try it.

Woman Two

I couldn't.

Man

I think you should.

Woman Two

Do you?

Man

I do.

Woman Two

You do.

Man

Try it. She can't you see.

I can tell that with her, compliance would be misunderstood. It would be difficult for her, she would think it a defeat.

Woman Two

What will she think?

He puts the necklace around her neck.

Man

Soft. So soft.

Woman Two

It's the bother of knowing what to wear being a woman. It is a bother you know, tell the gentleman nothing and to dress appropriately you know. It's such a bother, the business of clothes and dressing unless you are particular or want to please and very few of us do, yourself. I am not interested in that. It seems like vanity.

Man

There is no vanity in a woman dressing. She does it for a purpose more than vanity, surely. In men vanity is different, a way of telling one tosser from another tosser. In women it's quite different.

Your mother's vanity was part of her enchantment. That wasn't vanity. A vain woman would be an awful thing, if she was doing it with only herself to please. That's what plain women do affecting plain dress. Plain women in the right clothes can be quite another thing.

Woman Two

Now in a new dispensation we feel we can dress more appropriately.

Man

Clothes are a necessary part of the business. An acknowledgment of duty and understanding that being a woman involves men. It is a duty to herself, to what she is. A sign of compliance and a celebration, a rejection of the idea that dress is for other women. Like the duty a wife feels when she changes her pinny at teatime.

A mother teaches her daughter the ways of submission when she teaches her to braid her hair but a wise woman goes her own way with her clothing after that. It's a sign of maturity when you stop dressing to please your mother. If your mother likes what you wear or if your husband likes you in what your mother likes there is something wrong with the set-up. The emancipated woman is always hated by her sisters, always ugly.

Shaving the cunt obviates the need to shave the head. It's all about a suitable compliance.

She was so well-calculated you see. Nothing overdone but more to the point nothing underdone. Oh the smell of her. A woman who is discreet with her make-up or dresses to suit another woman, whose hair is dyed to please her sister or dresses in loose clothes or wears a soft chignon has no understanding of what men are.

Woman Two

We're too old for that now and besides the bother.

Man

Not too old. A woman too old? No. Many a good tune played on an old fiddle, age is but a number, there's good wine in old bottles. There's a special sweetness to an old lady that is only understood by the few who know.

Woman Two
And how found us?

Man
Some research asking in the public house and in the church. Asking around.

SCENE NINE

The Man and the two Women, Woman One with the beer.

Woman Two
You found it. Good. In the larder was it? I knew we must have some still.

Woman One
Yes.

Woman Two
I was certain. Keeping it cool, that's what we thought. Is that where it was? Will you have a glass? I thought we had some. But will it be cold enough for you though, I wonder?

Man
I'm sure it will be.

Woman Two
What is it, dear? What are you saying? What are looking like that for?

(*Acknowledging the necklace.*) Oh, I am sorry. Oh dear.

(*Taking it off.*) I am sorry, dear, I should have asked if you minded. Do you mind?

Woman One
Don't take it off on my account.

44

Woman Two
No, no. I will, I will.

Man
Leave it. Leave it. Don't take it off.

Woman Two
No. No. It's your turn you put it on.

Man
It's nice to see it worn.

Woman One
It never will be after this, if I am a judge.

Woman Two
What? Do you think? Why?

Woman One
You have it, dear. I don't mind you know, really.

Woman Two
It's so pretty, won't you try it? Try it, dear. It will look much nicer on you.

Woman One
No, thank you.

Man
You're so big sister. She was just pleasing me, is all.

Woman One
I am sure she was.

Woman Two
Now now, dear.

Woman One
You have a flush to the cheek and a sparkle to the eye.

Man
It is nice to be pleased.

Woman Two

You are trying to put a difference between us. Own it you are.

Woman One

Pour the beer.

Woman Two

Shall I? I can pour the beer. Watch me pour the beer. See. Into the side of the glass. My grandfather taught me to do it like this. He liked pale ale, Worthington E. I hope you like it. We got it in for Mr Franks. But is it cold enough for you? Such a very nice man, often our saviour in times past, when we needed help. But you see I thought you . . . I did silly, that you . . . silly, silly . . .

Woman One

You didn't think any such thing.

Woman Two

I did. I did, dear.

Woman One

Is that all right, is it cool enough for you?

Man

Oh yes. Cool, but not too cold.

Woman Two

Oh good.

Man

Are you anxious? Am I making you anxious? Am I? The two of you nervous . . . not intended.

Woman One

Always when entertaining there can be uncertainty? Perhaps you would like a sandwich. Perhaps he would like a sandwich. Shall I make him a sandwich?

Woman Two
Would you like a sandwich? Oh do. She cuts the bread so thin.

Woman One
I can certainly make a sandwich if you would like one. Would you like a sandwich?

Woman Two
Oh, do.

Man
No, no. This is fine, it really is.

Woman One
Put that in its case, dear, out of the way now.

Woman Two
Are you sure you don't want to try it on?

Woman One
No, no, no.

Woman Two
Won't you? Look, it's so pretty.

Woman One
Let me see it.

Man
That's it.

Woman Two
Go on.

Woman One
It is lovely. Do you mind?

Man
I led her astray, you see.

Woman One
Yes, putting on a jade necklace. What next!

Woman Two
You try it now.

Woman One
Will I?

Woman Two
Yes, your turn. Oh yes. Do, do.

Man
Here, let me.

Woman One
I'll do it, thank you.

Man
What a difference between you. So independent the one.

Woman One
I can't do it up. Could you?

Man
Let me, let me, there we are, you see. There we are. Share and share.

Woman Two
Nice. Lovely, it looks lovely.

Woman One
I don't like it. Doesn't suit. Take it off. Take it off. It's too tight. You have it.

She takes off the necklace.

Woman Two
Don't be ungracious, dear, it's not like you.

Man
What is the matter?

Woman One
There is nothing the matter. You have it. There.

Woman Two
There is something. Indeed there is.

Woman One
No dear, no dear. Please, you have it.

Woman Two
We could both wear it.

Woman One
It will never be worn, if I am the judge of anything.

Woman Two
Now, now.

Woman One
You have it then, honestly.

Woman Two
We can't have it, you see how it is.

Woman One
You have it. I mean it. Do, dear.

Woman Two
No no, dear. Oh you can be so difficult. You can.

Woman One
You see, I warned you. He is thriving on this. This is so provoking.

Woman Two
Dear, come, darling.

Woman One
I told you.

Woman Two
Why such a fuss? It's nothing darling.

Woman One
And this now. She sees that I'm upset and now she thinks, she's gone too far. I don't want it. I don't. You

don't believe me, do you? I really don't mind. Why don't you believe me? Why should I have to do this? I don't want it. I don't like wearing green, you know that.

She put her fingers in the cakes but this has nothing to do with that, nothing to do with it. So frail and pretty, dear, and never say boo to a goose, but she put her fingers in the cakes to mark which was hers, you did.

Woman Two
Well, really, dear.

Woman One
Yes, yes.

Woman Two
Dear.

Woman One
She's very like my father, you see. There was a duplicitous side he had which masculinity hides so easily, a very male kind of duplicity that finds deviousness easy, in a way different to a woman. And a woman is not so easily hoodwinked by another woman, you see, or is forgiven by her. We know how low we can stoop from our experience of ourselves.

Man
So you distrust men and suspect women. Is that the position of all unmarried ladies?

Woman One
Pretty much of all ladies with any experience of the world.

Man
What constitutes experience of the world, in your case in particular?

Woman One
A world of experience different to your own.

Man
And my experience is suspect, is it?

Woman One
It is different.

Man
How different?

Woman One
By being so.

Woman Two
You can be so judgemental, dear. I didn't put it on to tease you in any way, I really didn't. It was out of a request to. It was.

Woman One
No, I am sure you didn't, dear. I'm sorry. I don't know why I am so upset, I am sorry, dear.

Woman Two
You were very unpleasant, dear, to talk about Father in front of someone who knew him to be so. Indeed thought him to be . . . knew him to be kind. He was dear, really he was. You know he was.

Man
He called you his little princesses. He did, always.

Woman One
Did he then? Did he? Well, Mother hated all such names. But they came easily down there. Came easily to Grandfather. She thought them silly and vulgar, such names.

Woman Two
I liked them.

Woman One

Funny how Mother gave him tone and she from such a poor home if they were to be believed. And Grandfather so comfortable.

Woman Two

Don't dear. Don't talk of that. We were little princesses, dear.

Man

A different taste there, perhaps. Is that it? A different taste there than the one you have now. One that makes you so reined in. Down there they were not afraid of show, they wore it like tribal finery, like royalty for show they were, not afraid of gold.

Woman One

And yet she made us frightened of it all. Who had found it so alluring.

Woman Two

You think so?

Woman One

Indeed I do.

Woman Two

Let us talk about something else now, shall we? And not go to where we wish we hadn't ventured, where we can't get out as easily as we got in. Don't you think?

Man

No.

Woman Two

What is it that is so annoying you, dear? What is it that is exercising you, dear? It's not how we remember it or felt about it, dear, but he remembers it differently.

That is all and that is not as you would like it
remembered.

Woman One
No.

Woman Two
Well dear, let it be.

Woman One
I only can recall unease and fear and not knowing,
that went with the vivacity he wants to recall.

The atmosphere always in the house and in the street
with only Mother different from it to protect us from
it and give us comfort. Almost ribald and violent,
something hardly denied, colours that if they were
expressed would be bright and primitive. Yet
everything remained black and white.

Violence that was barely suppressed, like a woman
pulling hair from the head in revenge – you heard of
that. All so male and female and unmediated. Oh
intense. And the men, too much in focus. Grandfather
sending a man to bring us home wherever we were,
often quite near. Always escorted home, like girls with
a destiny, like the foreign girls with their brothers
coming for them or their cousins. They thought it
charming and old-fashioned, a kind of gallantry.

Brothers coming for the girls, their cousins escorting
them and the sullen girls with their hot breath and the
boys' laughter and eyes flashing, so potent and
breathing such hot breath.

I remember one girl was sent away, back to the
mother country and worse, for we didn't know what.
Talk of killing her and how would we manage when
what was coming would come like death, unable to

entertain even the possibility of it for real, whatever it was.

And fear of the men, of the danger that was somehow part of things. A sense of their having something in mind for us that we never understood and which they never brought about.

Woman Two

Sandwich? Would you like a sandwich perhaps with the beer?

Man

Go on, I like to hear women talking. My drink loosening your tongues. Is it that?

Woman Two

Dear, you warned us of the possibility of indiscretion. We have a nccd to be discreet.

Woman One

He is hoping for indiscretion. I think he is seeking it from us now he has found us again. He wants the truth about us now he has found us again, what he thinks of as the truth. Or the consequence of hiding the truth, of not acknowledging it, is that it?

Man

Is that what I am doing?

Woman One

He expects to find that we are disappointed women, isn't that it? And to pick at the shame of our being so, to see us pick at the scab of our shame, to assume that no matter what the matter is as experienced by us – because our life looks something static to him. Our life looks a poor thing, is that what he thinks?

Woman Two

Dear, really.

Woman One

Relative to the world as he knows it, in comparison to it.

Woman Two

What is the matter with you?

Woman One

He sees us as stopped, stopped. Our maturing or flowering, as stopped, and not what was proposed.

Like characters in a comedy of disappointed women. He sees that some women remain spinsters even in marriage and he sees us as if we were paralysed so now we are paralysed, you see, in comparison to the world you have allowed in here. Do you see? In a get-up-and-go world. Paralysed. Like we have had a stroke, in part paralysed.

Woman Two

We are not paralysed. I refuse to accept that. Why are you saying such a thing?

Woman One

It would seem like that to him, dear. That is what we are. Is that it? Lives like ours easy to describe. We are completely stuck in their fixing of us, our life here you see, dear. Here in a world we made private.

All children make up for their mother's pain. It's common enough. Whether it's the pain of an unfaithful husband or worse. He comes from a world where bad things happen to other people, where they bank on nothing happening to them. They bank that their child will be fine, that they won't lose their employment or be left or deserted, that those things will happen to other people knowing well they will happen to someone. But they live in hope it won't be them.

Woman Two

But dear, what are you saying, why are you fussed by it, dear? Look what we have got, dear. Look at you, dear. You are such a dear and look at what we learned from her. We got all that from her, from her. How talented you are. That basket you put flowers in for the Christmas table that was so tasteful and so inventive. She is so inventive. She is. She has Mother's taste and she makes life so graceful and it's all because of her efforts that it is so, not mine.

I am a dreamer she says, plump and indolent, content to feed the birds. That is why we live so well in our little house, that was up to you dear. And what could they have done without you? It was no mean feat, and you such a beauty, your talent for figures and you were enterprising then in the trouble, you negotiated all of the selling and saved them with your practicality. Mother had so much ambition for you. That you would marry a chartered accountant or become a secretary. But that's another thing and there we are. I am content, truly, dear.

Woman One

But dear, your sweetness, he has come to relish his memories of what it was for him. Romance of what it was, that is gone anyway. He wants to hear stories that hold no charm for us. For me at any rate.

Barroom stories of life down there. Of waterfront life. The story of the man, of two men, a big man and a little man, drinking in the same bar, when the one man, the little man, was so argumentative, was so provoking, that the big man picked him up, the little man, neck and crop, and threw him out of the open door across the road into the bar of the public house on the other side of the street, without caring for the traffic.

It was perhaps the same man, a big man, a sailor, a Swedish sailor, as it was told, who tormented by perhaps by the same little man, perhaps, who was wanting a fight. Like a fly around him and looking to fight and who the big man, the Swede, ignored and ignored, but who provoked the Swede so much, goaded him so much, but to no effect it seemed, in pubs and bars along the waterfronts of two towns. Until at last, driven too far, the gentle Swede bent down and bit off his tormentor's nose.

Was it he who told of sailing into Archangel before the mast in a whaling ship? Of the hard life then?

And stories of women. Of the woman whose husband brought no money in and who was unfaithful to her to boot and so cocksure of himself, a dandified rascal. So she, poor coloured woman, driven beyond endurance, she cooked molasses in a saucepan and when next he came strutting in, she threw the scalding mess into his face.

Or of you at the mission for sailors flirting with the sailors until you were stopped. Bringing home the young man who sat with his legs open wearing a too big signet ring, that they stopped that too. And stopping my marrying for they thought no one was suitable.

Man
Wear it, please wear it. She doesn't want it. Put it around your neck again please.

Woman Two
No no.

Man
Your skin is so soft.

Woman Two
No.

Woman One

We're shot of that, that, that rackety bohemian past,
that immigrant past. We have moved on you see. You
want us to remain where we were to suit you. But we
want rid of all that seaport, that waterfront,
docklands – all that. Reminding us of what denies us
our own feeling. All that lace and religious
processions and olive oil and spices and things alien to
us now. The locking prayer books and long rosary
beads and mantillas, all the mother of pearl and
coloured Easter eggs and Arab festivals, and the
virgins with oriental eyes, smell of leather and gold
and market vegetables and gold and men's tattoos and
coloured men laughing and okra and salt fish, like a
Mardi Gras stalking all over. We claim citizenship
here. We want shot of it. We have no diasporic longing
except of our own. You think that you can return us
to it. We have our own ache.

Woman Two

Well then, have you finished your beer? I expect you'd
better be going. It must be time.

Man

Well, I'd better go now.

I'll go. No place for me here is there?

Woman One

Indeed.

Woman Two

Have you finished your beer?

Man

True, she's true, you're true. Your grandfather was a
foreign-looking old crook, a Maltese-looking old
ringed greasy old foreigner with his counting-house
ways like an old Jew with his bag of money. Perhaps

he was an old Jew. Were you the grandchildren of an old Jew who gave me sixpence? And your father was a poor second to the old fraud who sent me to sea and the old witch with a tarot pack with her crocodile tears was a mean-spirited old biddy.

But she transfigured it like a queen. She made it into a Balkan romance, she turned it into an Italian film, she infused it with a Russian sweetness and an English gentility. She brought it out of Africa into Europe. She redeemed it with her poise. She was the mediator. She was the queen. Oh yes.

Don't you see the man she would make you? I wish I had oh something of hers. I wish I had kept something, taken something that she wore as a comfort, from her underclothes, even one of her little dainty little handkerchiefs. She was always pleasant. Her big silly sad eyes her kindness her ready laughter her compassion her style. I was seeking out for the secret the secret under the powder. Her cunty smell under it, seeking her cunty smell I knew must be there under the scent of her powder. I wanted to be tested by such a women, risk being thrown on to any rocks she hid and guarded. Are you wet still, do you get wet still? I like your soft skin, wrinkled skin. Not to speak of her compliance like a goddess. I am disappointed in you.

Woman One
He is like a cuckoo, he has returned to find an empty nest, to find it empty. We have gone. You were preposterous, a needy little runt, a little inconsequential walk-on, an addition, a pensioner, a duty an afterthought an eater of scraps. You dribble. Do you want his dribble? Posturing like some waterfront coloured man.

Woman Two

He's not a black man. You're not a black man.

Man

Well, I'll be on my way, thank you for the beer.

Woman Two

Yes, I think it's time, don't you think? Thank you for popping in.

Woman One

He goes now.

Woman Two

You must go, you see.

I have done as you ask, dear, you see.

Man

You were always too young or too old. Never quite what anyone wanted. Now, your skin in soft folds. If you knew how to look forward. Old cunt is much to be appreciated. All the boys now are after old cunt. They think far from finding it a convenience, see it as a luxury, in these times they can afford to think that. They like old darlings like you. Not my job to persuade you. No. Purely politesse. Purely social, just recording what is a fact. How much you could be desired. It was her I wanted to see. So I had better go. You are too proud.

Woman Two

Best that you go.

Woman One

Don't go on my account.

Man

You are not very gracious. She was very gracious, very gracious.

Woman One
Your beads.

He breaks up the jade necklace.

Woman Two
Goodbye.

He goes.

Well dear, there we are.

Nice to talk of old times.

Woman One
Nothing to do with us now, dear.

SCENE TEN

The Man alone in the hall.

Man
I'll be off then is that it? I am going then, OK? I'll say
bye-bye then shall I? Well, goodbye then. Yes? Yes?
Goodbye then. Into the world with me. Time to get
used to it again. Do you hear me? Pleasant meeting.
Off on my travels ah-ha.

*He goes out of the front door and as he closes it
behind him the back door into the kitchen opens and
the two women come in.*

Woman Two
Has he gone?

SCENE ELEVEN

*Woman Two alone in the kitchen, her hand on the open
door.*

Woman Two

He had such fond memories, dear. Of us in our ribbons. You always had such knots in your hair, dear. Is Mr Franks coming today I wonder? No you say and he was no bother and you got rid of him.

Are you there, dear?

SCENE TWELVE

Woman Two sitting looking out of the door, Woman One in front of the front door, as at the beginning.

Woman One

I am here dear. I am dear.

Are you in dear?

Dear? Are you dear?

What are you doing dear?

I am in dear.

Dear?

SCENE THIRTEEN

Woman Two alone, looking out of the back door.

Woman Two

Are you there dear?

I am here dear, just sitting dear, waiting for you dear.

Are you there dear?

Dear?

Dear?

Dear?

Will there be pain?

Dear?

Will there be time?

I will close the door now, dear.

Are you there, dear?

I'll close the door.

Dear?

She closes the door.

End.